Facing Yourself in the Bible

Studies of Bible Personalities

WILLIAM J. KRUTZA

CONTEMPORARY DISCUSSION SERIES

BAKER BOOK HOUSE
Grand Rapids, Michigan

Copyright 1976 by
Baker Book House Company
ISBN: 0-8010-5369-2
Printed in the United States of America

Scripture passages are from the Revised Standard Version of the Bible, Copyrighted 1946, 1952, 1971, 1973 by The National Council of the Churches of Christ. Used with permission.

CONTENTS

1 Getting Off the Hook.........*(Adam and Eve)* 7
2 Religious Phoneyism .... *(Cain)* 12
3 A Dominant Characteristic ....*(Jabez)* 17
4 Forging into an Unseen Future...... *(Abraham)* 21
5 Committed to Now ....*(Esther)* 26
6 Commitment to Care ....*(Ruth)* 31
7 I Do All the Work ....*(Martha)* 35
8 Disciple in Working Clothes......... *(Andrew)* 39
9 Contradictions ....*(Peter)* 43
10 Making Performance Match Beliefs ... *(Pharisees)* 47
11 Curious or Committed .... *(Zacchaeus)* 51
12 A New Direction................... *(Paul)* 55
13 Thank Quotients...............*(Ten Lepers)* 59

INTRODUCTION

I can never get away from the phrase in James 5:17 "Elijah was a man of like nature with ourselves" whenever I study the lives of biblical people. No biblical personages, outside of Jesus Christ, were superhuman even if they seemed to perform superhumanly on occasions.

Biblical people were human—as much as I am human. And in this I rejoice, not that I can find an excuse for my poor behavior, but that I can discover an understanding God and the source for inner strengths to live.

I take no comfort in the fact that some biblical characters did acts I'd never think of performing—murder, visiting prostitutes, torturing those who opposed them. I know that within every man is the capacity to indulge in some gross evil. I know I am not exempt from that capacity.

My love for the study of biblical personalities has led me to examine my own character and my reactions to the God who created me as a person. Like the biblical people who had life-changing encounters with God, I'm grateful for the possibilities still open to God to do his life-changing work in my life.

These discussions could be said to have originated in some of the struggles I have faced in life. Because I have encountered the God of these biblical people, I am better equipped to face life today. I hope that as you too face these people, meet their God, and look into the mirror of the Bible, you will be aware of possibilities for changing your own life and for meeting the challenges God places before you while you are being "conformed to the image of Jesus Christ."

1. Getting Off the Hook

But the Lord God called to the man, and said to him, "Where are you?" And he said, "I heard the sound of thee in the garden, and I was afraid, because I was naked; and I hid myself." He said, "Who told you that you were naked? Have you eaten of the tree of which I commanded you not to eat?" The man said, "The woman whom thou gavest to be with me, she gave me fruit of the tree, and I ate." Then the Lord God said to the woman, "What is this that you have done?" The woman said, "The serpent beguiled me, and I ate" (Gen. 3:9-13).

Have you ever noticed that even a young child will try to blame anything or anyone but himself for wrong conduct? Some fantisize. Others lie outright. But the intended result is the same—get off the hook, keep from being punished for wrongdoing.

This practice isn't a new psychological phenomena. We can't blame it on a permissive society. Nor is it limited to especially sinful people. It began in the Garden of Eden with the first humans, Adam and Eve.

Note the setting: Adam and Eve had already disobeyed God's command, "You may freely eat of every tree of the garden; but of the tree of the knowledge of good and evil you shall not eat, for in the day that you eat of it you shall die" (Gen. 2:16-17).

Let's not immediately condemn these early Garden dwellers. Had not God built into their personalities the powers of curiosity? Hadn't they exercised this by investigating the plant and animal world over which they were to have domain? And what precedent did they have to understand what God meant when he declared,

"For in the day that you eat of it you shall die"? Wasn't death an unknown?

Walking past that special "tree of the knowledge of good and evil"—whatever it looked like, and no doubt it had some distinctive features—must have at least aroused their curiosity. Can't you hear Adam and Eve questioning the significance of this special "no no" object in their midst!

Then came that will-shattering whisper from the serpent—and they indulged. Suddenly they "knew"! Suddenly they also understood the phenomenon of disobedience. And when God called to Adam, Adam had already invented a story to get himself off the hook.

Let's analyze his story. First, he recognized what had never been a problem before—his nudity. As soon as he heard God's voice, he became afraid and said, "I heard the sound of thee in the garden, and I was afraid, because I was naked; and I hid myself." Maybe this was his first "getting off the hook" statement. Rather than confessing disobedience, Adam grabbed the first seemingly logical explanation. He noticed he wasn't clothed, or protected by feathers or fur like some of the other creatures, so he hid.

But God knew this was a cover-up. And to force Adam to realize this, God asked, "Who told you that you were naked?" Then he got to the heart of the matter by asking the soul-penetrating question, "Have you eaten of the tree of which I commanded you not to eat?"

Sure enough, like many modern men, Adam had already figured out a way to get off that hook. He answered, "The woman whom thou gavest to be with me, she gave me fruit of the tree and I ate."

Notice that Adam was saying that God was partially at fault when Eve did wrong because God had created her. In the same way that a consumer accuses the designer when an appliance breaks down a couple of days after the guarantee runs out, so Adam pointed his finger toward the divine Designer: "There must have been something wrong when you put Eve together in the first place. This must be about the time the guarantee runs out!"

If that wasn't a sufficient argument for sinning, Adam turned the discussion toward his partner. He might have pointed at her when he exclaimed, "**She** gave me of the fruit of the tree and I did eat." That's cowardly innocence to say the least.

Have you ever been in a situation where a man blames his wife for his misdeeds? Has it ever happened in your home? How about sister-brother situations? "She did it!" "He did it!"

Seemingly the first one to make the accusation feels his conscience is cleared even though he is as guilty as the one he accuses.

We're not sure why God built into that first human the capacity (or weakness) which resulted in blaming someone outside of himself for his sin. Maybe it's because the positive side of that characteristic would have resulted in the power to resist the temptation. If Adam would have exercised this power, who knows what the world would be like today? At least he would have put the last statement first, "I ate." At least he would be taking full responsibility for his own acts.

Of course, Eve wasn't innocent on this score either. She took the same approach. While telling the truth that the temptation came via the serpent, she sought to get herself off the hook by stating, "The serpent beguiled me, and I ate."

Before condemning Adam and Eve, consider two factors. First, give them considerable credit for the powers of personality they must have possessed and expressed. As far as we can ascertain, they were fulfilling God's plan by having dominion over their natural surroundings. For example, animals were being named and tamed.

Secondly, consider our own propensity for covering our sins. Usually we cringe from any white lights shining on our souls. We don't like exposure, especially before the watching world.

It takes a mature character to say, "I did wrong; I have sinned; it's all my fault." But somehow this gets things running clockwise. It sets the sails into the most refreshing wind. It brings God's forgiveness and approval. It helps us stand tall among others, even though they've seen our darker side.

Shouldering full responsibility for one's own behavior is another aspect of the image of himself that God has built into humans. It's a mark of spiritual maturity. It evidences a proper psychological understanding of oneself. It indicates a desire to please God and to live honestly in the sight of all men, regardless of the cost.

The only proper way to get off the hook is through forgiveness—from both God and men!

FOR DISCUSSION

1. Discuss the ability (or weakness) of Adam and Eve to disobey God's command. Would you rather not have this personality trait yourself? Why, or why not?
2. Since God created man with the possibility of submitting to disobedience, can we in any way blame God for man's sinfulness? Why, or why not?
3. What within you as a person bends you to cover up wrongdoing?
4. Why are we so concerned about a good public image? Wouldn't it be easier to expose ourselves as we are rather than live a lie to ourselves and others?
5. I Corinthians 10:13 says: "No temptation has overtaken you that is not common to man. God is faith-

ful, and he will not let you be tempted beyond your strength, but with the temptation will also provide the way of escape . . . ." How does this apply to the temptation to cover up wrongdoing?

6. How can a person bring his public image more in line with his private practice? Is this a worthy aim for the Christian?

7. How could Paul's injunction "not to think of oneself more highly than he ought to think" be applied to the matter of a proper public image?

8. Since the practice of trying to get off the hook is often a subtle personality quirk, how does one overcome it? Is it sufficient to confess it to God? How does one "provide things honest in the sight of all men" and still hold the respect of others?

9. Are there any situations in which getting off the hook only makes you more responsible for your actions? Explain.

10. Give examples of any occasions when you should get others off the hook by taking blame that should rightfully fall to them?

11. The application of I John 1:9 remedies wrongdoing in God's sight. What other Scripture verses deal with this problem? What verses give instruction in how to overcome the problem in the presence of others?

2. Religious Phoneyism

In the course of time Cain brought to the Lord an offering of the fruit of the ground, and Abel brought of the firstlings of his flock and of their fat portions. And the Lord had regard for Abel and his offering, but for Cain and his offering he had no regard. So Cain was very angry, and his countenance fell. The Lord said to Cain, "Why are you angry, and why has your countenance fallen? If you do well, will you not be accepted? And if you do not do well, sin is couching at the door; its desire is for you, but you must master it" (Gen. 4:3-7).

Take a good look at the chapters preceding this passage. Is there any hint to suggest the type of sacrifice that would be pleasing in God's sight? If there was previous instruction, why doesn't the opening part of Genesis mention it? What biblical evidence do we have that sacrifices were a necessary part of worship at this time?

Nothing previous to this event gives any indication that either God or man had inaugurated a sacrificial system or a system of worship. It is poor hermeneutics to read back into this passage meanings which pertain to a sacrificial system instituted at a later date.

On the other hand, we do not have to deny the universal law so clearly depicted in the sacrificial system established under the law. The writer of Hebrews clearly stated its essence. "Indeed, under the law almost everything is purified with blood, and without the shedding of blood there is no forgiveness of sins" (9:22).

In seeking to understand why God found Cain's sacrifice unacceptable we must search the immediate passage. We cannot superimpose a future practice upon the text and easily conclude that Cain's presentation didn't meet the demands of the Mosaic law. However, Cain knew nothing of that law. Even that law allowed for sacrifices of vegetation.

Looking at this man's religious involvement from the viewpoint of our chapter title, we immediately discover why God found his sacrifice unacceptable. We also discover how easy religious phoneyism can creep into our lives—and, hopefully, how we can avoid it.

First, let's give Cain his due. He brought the first sacrifice recorded in the Bible. Presumably his interests were more inclined toward vegetables and fruits than toward animals. Nothing wrong in that. Why he chose gardening as a vocation can't be questioned. There was nothing more spiritual about Abel's sheep-tending. Doesn't worship include presenting to God the fruits of our labors as well as the thoughts of our minds and the words of our lips? If the answer is yes, then Cain qualified on this score.

In comparing the attitudes of Cain and Abel we discover why God favored Abel's sacrifice. We also discover the perils of religious phoneyism. From the description of Abel bringing the "firstlings of his flock," it seems that he took special care in what he presented to God. Also, the fact that he offered no resistance to Cain's attack indicates a certain innocence of nature—something acceptable to God. It would not do this passage an injustice to conclude that Abel was innocently honest with God.

The attitude of Cain does not bear similar earmarks. His reaction to God's disqualifying his sacrifice indicates a nature filled with hatred and envy. Cain reacts out of the nature of his being. How one thinks is a determining factor in how he will react to any negative or positive input. The bitterness within Cain exploded, portraying the real man!

With this dormant (or perhaps even conscious) attitude, Cain came with his bundle of vegetation to worship God. God's rejection of the fruit simply indicated the unacceptability of Cain. Cain had come as if nothing was wrong inside.

In our day and society, it is easy to go to church. Because of our affluence we too can "bring to the Lord an offering." We can participate in all the rituals of worship, including the uttering of prayers, the giving of money, and singing well-known melodies. To those observing our regular attendance, our participation in activities, and our financial assistance, we are acceptable.

But it is possible to go through religious motions when, deep within, our being is headed in another direction. Only God can detect religious phoneyism—whether in Cain or in William!

The Bible has much to say about religious phoneyism. In some instances, such as in Christ's dealings with the Pharisees, it is labeled pure hypocrisy. Note Christ's severe condemnations of hypocrites in Matthew 23:13-36. Ear-scorching words!

The Lord puts his finger on the root cause of religious phoneyism. " . . . This people draw near with their mouth and honor me with their lips, while their hearts are far from me, and their fear of me is a commandment of men learned by rote" (Isa. 29:13). Such words constitute a warning: Regardless of how orthodox our doctrine, if it is simply committed to memory without a corresponding change of life, we will be guilty of phoney religious worship. Worship must be "in spirit" as well as "in truth" as Jesus so aptly put it when speaking to the woman at the well (John 4:24).

David expresses this in two of his psalms. In Psalm 40:6-8 he declares: "Sacrifice and offering thou dost not desire; but thou hast given me an open ear. Burnt offering and sin offering thou hast not required. Then I said, 'Lo I come; in the roll of the book it is written of me; I delight to do thy will, O my God; thy law is within my heart," Then in Psalm 51:17, "The sacrifice acceptable to God is a broken spirit; a broken and contrite heart, O God, thou wilt not despise."

Jesus took this one step further—a common practice in His teaching. He declared that we don't even have a right to worship if we know that someone has something against us. He said, "So if you are offering your gift at the altar, and there remember that your brother has something against you, leave your gift there before the altar and go; first be reconciled to your brother, and then come and offer your gift" (Matt. 5:23-24).

FOR DISCUSSION

1. If we know that God "discerns my [our] thoughts from afar" (Ps. 139:2), why are we prone to make ourselves out to be more than we are?
2. Why do we so often seek the approval of men and thus present our better side?
3. We read in 1 Samuel 16:7, " . . . The Lord sees not as man sees; man looks on the outward appearance, but the Lord looks on the heart." If we understand this truth, will we be less conscious of making a good impression?
4. What are some of the things we consciously do to impress others with our spirituality?
5. What would happen in your church if suddenly each person became honest with God? What would happen in your community?
6. What significance should I John 1:9 have in altering our attitudes in worship?
7. How can we keep ourselves honest toward God and others and still express the proper Christian graces?

8. Are there any sins that should not be confessed in public? How does one determine how intimately he exposes his personality problems and conflicts in a group setting?
9. What are some basics that will keep us from becoming religious phonies while remaining orthodox in our beliefs?

3. A Dominant Characteristic

Jabez was more honorable than his brothers; and his mother called his name Jabez, saying, "Because I bore him in pain." Jabez called on the God of Israel, saying, "Oh that thou wouldst bless me and enlarge my border, and that thy hand might be with me, and that thou wouldst keep me from harm so that it might not hurt me!" And God granted what he asked (I Chron. 4:9-10).

When thinking of famous people, we often associate a term with their name. To mention a few: Stalin—brutal; Pope John—loving; Napoleon—conqueror; Billy Graham—dynamic; Einstein—brilliant. The list could go on and on. Through historical and biographical information we can easily discover the dominant characteristics of famous or infamous people. News media in our present era provide much information about present world personalities.

We can continue the exercise by turning to biblical characters: Abraham—faithful; Elijah—bold; Martha—serving; Andrew—doing the right thing at the right time.

We realize that stating one characteristic in a person's life doesn't provide much dimension. A closer look would indicate more than a one-sided person. Yet one characteristic was dominate in his life.

In the case of Jabez we learn that he was a praying man. That's all! And in the context of the Bible, that doesn't seem to be unique. Praying men are not a rarity in biblical settings.

Recall the thunderous prayer of Elijah when he challenged the prophets of Baal (I Kings 18:36-38).

Review the polished (and possibly premeditated) prayer of Solomon at the dedication of the Temple (I Kings 8:22-53). Visualize king-defying Daniel on his knees three times a day before an open window (Dan. 6:10). Recall the agonizing session of the Savior in Gethsemane (Matt. 26:39-44) or Stephen's cry at his death (Acts 7:55-60). Compare the heavenward utterances of the Pharisee and the publican (Luke 18:9-14).

So what's different about Jabez? He's mentioned only in these two verses in the Bible. We know nothing else about him. We know that his mother had considerable pain during his birth and named him in memory of that agony. But other than this, we know little. We can assume that he was a landowner. He asked God to "enlarge his borders."

The other two portions of his prayer are generalizations. He asked that God's hand be with him—something that each individual can explain only within the context of personal experience. Secondly, he asked to be kept from harm. In an undeveloped agricultural society in the extremely hilly land of Palestine, this could have been a cry for protection against wild animals or ruthless, nomadic plunderers.

To these simple requests came a satisfying reply. The text clearly states, "And God granted what he asked." How beautiful! How character revealing—both of God and of Jabez.

So in the long line of genealogies, Jabez seemed to be a special kind of man. The distinction of uttering at least one prayer that brought God's intervention into the human scene is Jabez's only claim to fame. Being known throughout history as a praying man sets him apart from most of his contemporaries. At least no mention is made of their prayer feats.

Of course, prayer is not an isolated action. He did not have to bother praying for an enlargement of his property or for protection if he wasn't an involved person. Prayer was a natural outgrowth of his involvement in his personal and social surroundings. He probably was a busy man, so prayer wasn't a substitute for involvement. Nothing is even said about gathering his family into the prayer circle to consult God on a matter that surely was of interest and concern to them. He didn't seem to be in any particular place when he called upon God, and the prayer was not made at a large public meeting.

Only a few people are aware of their dominant characteristics. Often others recognize these good qualities and point them out to us in a direct or indirect way. Once we are aware of our good traits, it is up to us to decide how to use them in a humble, yet positive way. To exercise our personal power points in an unassuming manner enhances the values of these good traits.

Jabez probably was not aware that others noticed he had prayed. Only after his bones began to return to the dust was his name put on the list of praying men.

This leads to a serious question. Should we recognize our own dominant characteristics? One would immediately say yes if that recognition resulted in our changing those characteristics for the better or using them more efficiently to glorify God. However, to be recognized by others can develop into an inner battle with humility—a virtue that we'll immediately lose if we recognize it in ourselves.

There's a place for honest self-evaluation and recognition of strong characteristics which we've inherited or developed. In fact, this brings us up to the position in which we were created: "a little less than God ... crowned ... with glory and honor" (Ps. 8:5). Properly developing and using our recognized characteristics must result in the good of others and the glory of God.

FOR DISCUSSION

1. How should one go about discovering his dominant characteristics—those that seem to be expressed most often? If these are good, what should be the next step? If they are bad, how can they be corrected?
2. How does the transforming power of Jesus Christ affect one's personal characteristics? Describe some of the changes that took place in your life when you became a Christian.
3. When Paul talks about us being "new creatures" and that "old things have passed away," is he referring to changes in one's personality? If so, what kind of changes?
4. How can an analysis of the dominant characteristics of members of a congregation be useful in the ministry of a church? How can they be discovered?
5. What values do you discover in studying the lives of biblical people? historical people? people of today? Have you discovered that people haven't changed in their basic characteristics? What does this tell us about men? What can we learn from it?
6. If you are totally honest with yourself, what do you see as your dominant characteristic? Do you usually express it in a helpful manner? Why, or why not? Would you reveal it to others? Why, or why not?
7. How can these and other personal characteristics be channeled into useful activities to glorify God?
8. If you discover some unpleasant characteristic in another person, how should you react? How do you usually react?

4. Forging into an Unseen Future

Now the Lord said to Abram, "Go from your country and your kindred and your father's house to the land that I will show you. And I will make of you a great nation. ... So Abram went, as the Lord had told him; and Lot went with him. Abram was seventy-five years old when he departed from Haran (Gen. 12:1-2, 4).

By faith Abraham obeyed when he was called to go out to a place which he was to receive as an inheritance; and he went out, not knowing where he was to go. ... For he looked forward to the city which has foundations, whose builder and maker is God (Heb. 11:8,10).

John, a Christian, was satisfied with his job. It demanded enough creativity to challenge his mind. It provided an adequate salary plus several fringe benefits. The prestige of being at the management level appealed to his ego. He could expect a promotion in a year or two. Security, satisfaction, and the knowledge of supplying products beneficial to mankind's health made his job worthwhile.

Then a friend pleaded with John to go into a new business partnership, a high-risk venture. The benefits and salary would hinge upon John's performance. He'd have to forego job security. But the potential for growth and profit was appealing. Should he accept this challenge to go full force into an unseen future? How would you react?

Genesis 12 and Hebrews 11 put another famous biblical character into similar shoes. Abram (his name was later changed by God to Abraham in keeping with a promise to make him the father of a multitude of nations, Gen. 17:5), had a very comfortable situation in Haran. His father Terah had moved the entire family (and possibly clan) from Ur of the Chaldeans and settled in Canaan. At age 205 Terah died, leaving the inheritance to son Abram. Abram inherited considerable wealth.

Now at age seventy-five, Abram faces the opportunity and challenge to leave the security in hometown Haran and journey to an unknown future at an unknown place. There's only one different factor between modern John and ancient Abram? Or is there?

Our text proclaims the fact that "the Lord said to Abram." Most evangelicals have interpreted such phrases to mean a direct divine verbalization understandable by the individual involved. A few have interpreted such passages with caution, sometimes suggesting that a human mediator brought the message.

There may be some credence to this second interpretation in Abram's case. Hebrews 11 talks about his great faith. It wouldn't take much faith to respond to the known voice of deity. One could readily separate it from all human voices and immediately respond. Who wouldn't jump at the opportunity to respond to the literal voice of God? This wouldn't call for the kind of faith Hebrews 11:1 describes as hoping for and certain of what we *do not* see.

Whatever means of communication God used, obeying his command required what we call genuine faith. Abraham had to head full force into an unseen and unknown future. He had no more guarantees than would our modern John going into the high-risk business venture.

Is it possible that faith and high-risk have something in common? It seems that Abraham, along with several of the other biblical characters listed in the faith squad of Hebrews 11 (Jacob, Joseph, Moses, the people standing at the Red Sea's water edge, Joshua at Jericho, Rahab welcoming the spies, Gideon and his 300, Samson) had the ability to take a high risk.

God doesn't seem to commit much to the unadventurous! He knows who will and who will not launch out into the unknown. He spots men of faith and places a considerable challenge before them, a challenge that doesn't come in a neatly described plan or fully packaged. There is always a risk factor to faith, not a risk as to the trustworthiness of God, but a risk as to the involvement of the one called.

Abraham took the risk. He launched out. He left the familiar and journeyed into the unfamiliar. He left the secure and faced what could possibly end in insecurity. He pictured an inheritance which couldn't be put in legal terms. He looked forward when others his age (75 years) would have been content to nostalgically review the past.

Every man has opportunity to commit himself to the high-risk calls of God. God communicates such risks, calls to faith, so that we depend on the Lord. It's his way of testing our character and challenging us to greater adventures. Like Abraham, each of us has the opportunity to accept the challenge. In the end, God secures that to which he calls us. Whether we realize it or not, we obtain an inheritance. The results of faith are rewarding in this life and in the life to come.

FOR DISCUSSION

1. Describe some of the calls God gave to men in biblical times. Were these actual verbalizations? Could these calls be interpreted as coming through human mediators or prophets?

Recall the call of God to the boy Samuel (I Samuel). How do you explain this experience? Was Eli in tune enough spiritually to really recognize that God was calling to Samuel, or was he simply "getting himself off the hook"? Give reasons for your answer.

2. How does one make sure that what he has determined to be God's plan truly is God's plan?

3. If what we consider to be God's plan does not materialize, how does one explain the situation? Can we ever say that God changes his mind?

4. Do you believe God tailors his calls to one's capacities and character? Why, or why not? Does this help to explain why each person seems to get individual leading by God?

5. Some people seem quite free in telling how the Lord led them here or there. How do you react to such accounts? How can these people be sure that their actions aren't personal choice?

6. Is it possible for two people to claim the Lord's leading and end up with diametrically opposite viewpoints? How would you determine if either or both are doing the Lord's will?

7. Do you believe Christians sometimes use the idea of the Lord's leading as a justification for action? as a personal morale builder? as an unconscious or conscious means of demonstrating their spirituality?

8. At what point does our present knowledge of psychological reactions and mental abilities enter into the process of ascertaining God's will?

9. Do you sense a calling to greater risk-taking (biblical faith) in your own life? If so, in which areas? How do you personally assure yourself you are going where and how God desires?

10. How do you keep yourself from making unwise decisions that later prove to yourself and others more a

misappropriation of faith than an appropriation of this characteristic?

5. Committed to Now

And Mordecai told him all that had happened to him, and the exact sum of money that Haman had promised to pay into the king's treasuries for the destruction of the Jews. Mordecai also gave him a copy of the written degree issued in Susa for their destruction, that he might show it to Esther and explain it to her and charge her to go to the king to make supplication to him and entreat him for her people . . . . Then Esther spoke to Hathach, gave him a message for Mordecai, saying, ". . . if any man or woman goes to the king inside the inner court without being called, there is but one law: all alike are to be put to death, except the one to whom the king holds out the golden scepter that he may live . . ." Then Mordecai told them to return answer to Esther, "Think not that in the king's palace you will escape any more than all the other Jews. For if you keep silence at such a time as this, relief and deliverance will rise for the Jews from another quarter, but you and your father's house will perish. And who knows whether you have not come to the kingdom for such a time as this?" . . . "hold fast on my behalf . . . Then I will go to the king, though it is against the law; and if I perish, I perish" (Esther 4:7-16).

The average man on the street believes the main values of the church are futuristic. The phrase "pie in the sky" aptly illustrates the world's concept of the church's message. Such an evaluation has considerable validity. Far too often the life after death aspects of the believer's relationship to Christ have been presented so loudly and graphically that even the believer has missed much of the here-and-now quality of the gospel's message.

This is indeed unfortunate for both the world and the believer. The here-and-now aspects of God's message appear again and again on the pages of the Bible, regardless of which version one reads.

The dramatic story of Esther's call to appear before King Ahasuerus on behalf of the Jewish people is one of these here and now messages.

You will recall that Haman had continually schemed to eliminate his chief nemesis, Mordecai. Mordecai would not "bow down and do obeisance" (Esther 3:2) to Haman. He would not listen to the king's servants who presented Haman's demands. The Jew Mordecai revealed his nationality when he justified his position.

Since Haman couldn't get compliance from Mordecai, he planned the annihilation of all the Jews. Haman cleverly presented the matter to the king, got the king to agree to an annihilation decree, and sent the decree through all the provinces (read Esther 3).

When Mordecai heard of it, he put on the typical mourning garb, went to the king's gate and mourned. Jews throughout the kingdom did likewise, "fasting and weeping and lamenting, and most of them lay in sackcloth and ashes" (4:3).

Esther's immediate response was to be ashamed of her cousin's appearance at the king's gate. "She sent garments to clothe Mordecai, so that he might take off his sackcloth, but he would not accept them" (4:4). She then sent a messenger to Mordecai to learn about his strange behavior. The messenger brought back a copy of the decree and a request from Mordecai that Esther entreat the king on behalf of her people.

Esther first responded in the predictable manner. She considered what would happen to her personally if she went to the king. Even though she had most favored

27

status, to defy the king could mean death. And like every red-blooded person, she didn't want to die. No, she wouldn't go in to the king without being asked.

Her cousin's reaction was almost immediate, "Think not that in the king's palace you will escape any more than all the other Jews" (4:13). That put things in a little different perspective.

We've probably all heard sermons on being willing to die for Jesus Christ. Either vocally or in personal thinking, we've made the ultimate dedication, "Lord, I'm willing to even die for you!" Fortunate for us, the Lord didn't present us with an opportunity to test our emotion-packed response as soon as we left church on that day.

Remember Peter. Jesus was betrayed. In speaking of his death, he told the disciples that he was going away, "Where I am going you cannot go." Peter confidently answers, "Lord, why cannot I follow you now? I will lay down my life for you" (John 13:36, 37).

Jesus' response was most piercing. That's the question we have to ask ourselves before we make similar rash commitments. "Will you lay down your life for me?" (John 13:38).

We all know that in a now encounter, Peter's commitment disappeared like water through a sieve. The emotionally based outburst wasn't stable enough to carry him through the next crisis.

Esther's true character came through. Rather than boasting of what she'd do, she prepared herself, asked for backing by all the Jews (including her cousin whom she misunderstood previously), and then determined to reverse the king's decree. What courage! "If I perish, I perish!" (Esther 4:16). This was the ultimate in commitment to the now.

Crises of all types abound in our world. These include not only morality problems, but also great physical distresses. In some areas of the world people face annihilation by hunger. In America, it's moral annihilation: the drug culture, pornography, injustices to minorities, and racism.

Maybe commitment to these now issues isn't as glamorous as Esther's commitment to saving the scattered Jews, but such commitment is as necessary. Who can better meet these crises than those who are possessed by the eternal love of Christ? Jesus pointed in two directions when summing up all moral law: "You shall love the Lord your God with all your heart, and with all your soul, and with all your mind. This is the great and first commandment. And a second is like it, you shall love your neighbor as yourself" (Matt. 22:37-39).

That love to our neighbors has everything to do with the here and now. It doesn't take much investigation to discover situations within our culture or within our immediate communities which test our character and commitment. Is there an Esther around?

FOR DISCUSSION

1. What were some of the factors in her early life that probably helped to develop Esther's strength of character? What does this say about the character of Mordecai?
2. To present Esther as a candidate for the king's harem to be used possibly as a prostitute by either the king or political visitors if she didn't qualify to be queen seems to be taking a high moral risk. Can this risk be justified in the light of the Jewish code of conduct with its emphasis on moral purity?
3. Does the silence of Esther and Mordecai (Esther 2:20) concerning her Jewishness set any type of precedence or example as to declaring one's religious beliefs? Are there appropriate times in which to keep our beliefs silent? Give examples.

4. Do you agree that evangelicals are often prone to unnecessarily wave the banner of their faith before the watching world when they offer to meet men's physical/social needs? What reasons would you give for this tendency?
5. Is there a superiority attitude of "we have the answers" or "Christ is the answer" often visible when help is given? How would you combat or minimize that attitude?
6. Why is it more difficult to commit yourself to here and now issues than to the more ultimate realities such as belief for eternity? Why does it seem easier to join Peter's "I'll even die for you" than to apply our Christianity in transforming real life situations?
7. After initial acceptance of Christ's provisions for life after death, doesn't commitment also involve here and now application of biblical truth? Why do we get more excited about prophetic discussions of future events than about how we can demonstrate the love of Christ in a needy world?
8. Discuss a number of ways in which Christians in your church and community can supply remedies to here and now problems in your society and community.

6. Commitment to Care

But Elimelech, the husband of Naomi, died, and she was left with her two sons. These took Moabite wives; the name of the one was Orpah and the name of the other Ruth. They lived there about ten years; and both Mahlon and Chilion died, so that the woman was bereft of her two sons and her husband. ... Naomi said to her two daughters-in-law, "Go, return each of you to her mother's house. May the Lord deal kindly with you. ... The Lord grant that you may find a home, each of you in the house of her husband. ... Turn back, my daughters, go your way, for I am too old to have a husband. ... Orpah kissed her mother-in-law, but Ruth clung to her. ... Ruth said, "Entreat me not to leave you or to return from following you; for where you go I will go, and where you lodge I will lodge; your people shall be my people, and your God my God; where you die I will die, and there will I be buried" (Ruth 1:3-17).

Because she wasn't a citizen of the country, even after meeting the residency requirements in Moab, Naomi would have had only a slim chance to qualify for entrance into one of the country's retirement homes (if there were such facilities in Moab). She'd have to sign over her inheritance papers to the government, make application, have an interview, and wait for her name to come up on a list after all citizens were taken care of. Slim chance!

But it seems that her sons, Mahlon and Chilion, wouldn't have it that way, anyway. They took her into their homes, possibly on a six-month-per-son basis. At least we can conclude that her two Moabite daughters-in-law were accustomed to having her around.

Then Naomi's two sons died, possibly the victims of an epidemic. That left her with her daughters-in-law. She realized they weren't legally responsible for her so she'd have to return to relatives in Bethlehem and depend on the Jewish social security system.

Naomi sat down to discuss her plans with Orpah and Ruth. She encouraged them to go back to their mothers, find men to marry and establish homes, and worship according to the dictates of their religion. That sounded good to Orpah (who may have had some hang-ups about supporting her Jewish mother-in-law for the past ten years anyway). Orpah kissed Naomi good-by and went home. That was her legal privilege. She was not under any obligation to support her mother-in-law.

Ruth, however, went far beyond her legal responsibility. Even a justifiable moral response could have been limited to taking care of Naomi in Moab. "Why don't we stay together here? I'll get a job and we'll make out okay." But Ruth was willing to turn away from any family connections and even her religion in order to provide for Naomi. Her devotion to her mother-in-law seemed to mean more to her than devotion to her own mother and to the religion of the Moabites.

In our American culture we seemingly develop more Orpahs than Ruths. The problems of the aged are becoming larger every year. The Orpahs, who know their personal legal rights and lack a feeling of moral responsibility even for their fellow family members, tend to say the aged should be taken care of at governmental expense. That's what social security is all about, isn't it?

As new ways to cure diseases and to promote healthful living are discovered, the number of people beyond retirement age increases. In fact, with the birthrate near a population increase of zero percent, those past age sixty-five will soon make up one of the largest segments of the population.

Added to this increase of retirees is the American family attitude of independence. Many parents reflect the attitude that after their children become self-sufficient, self-supporting members of society, the parents don't want any responsibilities for other family members, young or old. Thus more retirement and convalescent homes are developed, places where the elderly can live comfortably . . . and by themselves. Any responsibility for them seems to be limited to occasional visits and the signature on a check.

Our text tells us something about the character of Ruth. Surely she didn't know what her commitment to her mother-in-law involved. Yet out of love and devotion she was ready to assume whatever responsibilities would come. She took a poor-paying, back-bending job when they got back to Bethlehem. "She set forth and went and gleaned in the field after the reapers" (Ruth 2:3).

Romance added a delightful touch to Ruth's story. She came to the attention of one of Naomi's husband's rich relatives. After a next-of-kin inheritance and marriage clearance (Ruth 3:1—4:10), Boaz married Ruth. After Ruth gave birth to a son, Naomi rejoiced even more because the inheritance would be intact. Ruth had no way of knowing what happiness awaited her when she made the initial commitment to one who could have easily been put on the unwanted relative list. The love bond between Ruth and Naomi was strong even without any hope of a comfortable life for Ruth. Love binds people together without any hope of self gain. It was that love which motivated Ruth to sacrifice personal gain for Naomi's good.

FOR DISCUSSION

1. How do you evaluate Ruth's commitment to Naomi?

Would such a commitment be possible and advisable in similar circumstances in our culture?

2. Can we develop any standards of conduct whereby we take responsibility for relatives left alone? Is there any obligation beyond legal obligations? Explain.
3. Even though many elderly people proclaim that they want to live by themselves, should the church seek to reverse this attitude and encourage the idea of living in with children? How would you promote this?
4. Since we are witnessing such a proliferation of retirement facilities which often outclass our home arrangements, what ought our attitudes be toward placing elderly parents in such surroundings?
5. If we would develop a commitment similar to Ruth's toward our elderly relatives, would we be justified in opposing governmental programs for senior citizens? Why, or why not?
6. Discuss various ways people in your community are fulfilling responsibilities toward senior citizens. Do these activities include elderly people living, perhaps alone, at home? What programs can be developed to encourage families to adopt Ruth-type commitments?

7. I Do All the Work

Now as they went on their way, he entered a village; and a woman named Martha received him into her house. And she had a sister called Mary, who sat at the Lord's feet and listened to his teaching. But Martha was distracted with much serving; and she went to him and said, "Lord, do you not care that my sister has left me to serve alone? Tell her then to help me." But the Lord answered her, "Martha, Martha, you are anxious and troubled about many things; one thing is needful. Mary has chosen the good portion, which shall not be taken away from her" (Luke 10:38-42).

From the beginning, even before man sinned, work has been an integral part of God's plan for humanity. After God created male and female, Genesis 1:28 states, "God blessed them, and God said to them, 'Be fruitful and multiply, and fill the earth and subdue it; and have dominion over . . . ' " In Genesis 2:15, "The Lord God took the man and put him in the garden of Eden to till and keep it." Notice the various expressions for the expending of human energy: be fruitful, fill the earth, subdue it, have dominion over, to till, and keep it. All these terms either imply or directly state that man was to work. Work was the means by which man accomplished God's purpose.

To work is to follow in God's pattern. Genesis 2:2 states; "And on the seventh day God finished his work which he had done." The fourth commandment contains these positive words, "Six days you shall labor, and do all your work" (Exod. 20:9). On many occasions the psalmist exulted in the working processes of God: "When I look at thy heavens, the work of thy fingers" (8:3); "The heavens are telling the glory of God; and the firmament proclaims his handiwork" (19:1); "O Lord how manifold are thy works! In wisdom hast thou made them all; the earth is full of thy creatures" (104:24).

In the great prayer of Moses recorded in Psalm 90, he pleads, "Let the favor of the Lord our God be upon us, and establish thou the work of our hands upon us, yea, the work of our hands establish thou it."

Paul reminds us in Ephesians 2:10 "For we are his workmanship, created in Christ Jesus for good works, which God prepared beforehand, that we should walk in them." To correct those who broke the eighth commandment "Thou shalt not steal," Paul gave these instructions to Ephesian converts: "Let the thief no longer steal, but rather let him labor, doing honest work with his hands" (Eph. 4:28). To the Colossians he wrote, "Whatever you do in, word or deed, do everything in the name of the Lord Jesus, giving thanks to God the Father through him" (Col. 3:17). He instructed the Thessalonians "to aspire to live quietly, to mind your own affairs, and to work with your hands, as we charged you; so that you may command the respect of outsiders, and be dependent on nobody" (I Thess. 4:11,12).

Surely Martha was well aware of the biblical concepts of the value of work. But even though one might have his head screwed on properly when it comes to theories of labor, he can easily get a cocked head by noticing that someone nearby seems to get by without too much work. In this case, Jesus Christ was commending Mary for not working at that hour. She, according to him, had chosen "the good portion," that of paying attention to the honored guest.

Martha was doing commendable work, but at the wrong time, and possibly out of the wrong motivation.

She was uptight with much serving. She had to prepare the food. She had to set the table. She had to clean the floor. She had to tidy up the room.

All the while Mary sat, drinking in the words of Jesus. Martha couldn't stand it. Her hostility spewed out, "Lord, don't you care that my sister has left me to serve alone? Tell her then to help me."

Jesus does not downgrade a neat, clean home and nourishing food tastily prepared. He does not advocate living in a simulated pigpen. Surely he was pleased to be in a relatively tidy setting. But he pointed out to Martha that her psychological attitudes were twisted and she was emotionally uptight. (Notice she didn't state she was tired, nor did Jesus suggest she needed to rest.) Jesus analyzed her emotional state, "Martha, Martha, you are anxious and troubled about many things." It wasn't rest she needed; it was a relaxed attitude even in the busyness of everyday living.

Beyond this, Jesus challenged her priorities. Surely everything she worked at so diligently had its place. But such work had to be placed in proper perspective. And it is here that we often get our priorities mixed. It is difficult to know which temporal labors have lasting or eternal significance. When does the temporal have a tinge of the eternal?

By proclaiming "I have to do all the work around here," Martha probably overstated her case. We often do this when we think our load is too heavy or some other person's load is too light. An analysis of the situation would probably reveal we were poor planners or we wanted recognition that was being given to others.

FOR DISCUSSION

1. If we take this situation out of the context of the Bible, what could we conclude about mundane work? Would this be fair?
2. How does one formulate a Christian concept of

work? What does this include? (It would be good to list several biblical ideas.)
3. Martha has often represented work and Mary worship. Should these be put in opposition? How would you harmonize these two human activities?
4. Describe any situations where the emphasis on work and worship would be reversed. Should work ever take precedence over worship?
5. Since almost all men, Christians included, are forced by social and economic pressures to spend most of their time in daily work, how can this allotment of time be justified in the light of what we believe to be eternal? Does temporal work have eternal values? Define.
6. A housewife spends considerable time preparing food, cleaning, washing clothes. What do all these activities have to do with eternity? With eternal rewards?
7. How should we view the amount of work done by others? Is there ever a time when we should compare it with our personal output?
8. Why is attitude so important in what we do? Would it be right to conclude that attitude in the job is of greater significance than the end results? Is any work ever mundane for the Christian?
9. Should each person develop a priority list of tasks to be performed either on his regular job or in relationship to his after-the-job-time? Make some listings and discuss why the items on the list are important in fulfilling eternal values.

8. Disciple in Working Clothes

One of the two who heard John speak, and followed him, was Andrew, Simon Peter's brother. He first found his brother Simon, and said to him, "we have found the Messiah" (which means Christ). He brought him to Jesus. (John 1:40-42).

Lifting up his eyes, then, and seeing that a multitude was coming to him, Jesus said to Philip, "How are we to buy bread, so that these people may eat?" ... One of his disciples, Andrew, Simon Peter's brother, said to him, "There is a lad here who has five barley loaves and two fish; but what are they among so many?" (John 6:5-9).

Now among those who went up to worship at the feast were some Greeks. So these came to Philip, who was from Bethsaida in Galilee, and said to him, "Sir, we wish to see Jesus." Philip went and told Andrew; Andrew went with Philip and they told Jesus" (John 12:20-22).

Being Simon Peter's brother could be something of which someone could be both proud and ashamed. Simon had an innate ability for coming up with stupendous thoughts or scatterbrained ideas. He could loudly proclaim "You are the Christ" and also suggest constructing a couple makeshift worship booths on the Mount of Transfiguration. He could boast of never denying the Lord and soon afterwards utter curses about Christ.

There was Andrew in the background, one time proudly telling his friends and another time wanting a place to hide when he said, "That's my brother."

In a sense it's a tragedy that almost every time the scripture writers identified Andrew, they indentified him as Simon Peter's brother. Andrew was a genuine person in his own right—one from whom we can learn much, one of whom we'd find many duplicates in our society. Unfortunately it's the Peters who get all the publicity. In fact, they seem to be their own PR agents.

If we'd give a surname to Andrew, it could be one of the following: Mr. Quiet Worker, Mr. Do, Mr. Shirtsleeve Disciple.

No matter where you read about Andrew, he's active. He's not in the limelight. His work is more significant than his presence. Yet he seems to be in a significant place doing a significant activity. He does not draw attention to himself. As far as Andrew was concerned, a follower of Jesus Christ expresses himself by what he does rather than by what he says. He let his boisterous brother be the mouthpiece of the family.

One can readily picture Andrew dressed in a working man's garb with his sleeves rolled up past the elbows. He's ready to do something for someone. Service was the great motivating force within his personality. And when he became a follower of the Savior, this motivation was at its highest and purest peak. It seems he delighted in bringing others to the Master without any regard for personal recognition.

His first act was to tell talkative Peter about the Messiah. Next, Andrew insisted that Peter have a personal encounter with the Lord.

On an occasion when 5000 people got so wrapped up in listening to Jesus that they became hungry, Andrew spotted a boy with a lunch bag. It contained five barley rolls and two dried fish. He was dubious about their value to Jesus, yet he made the fact known. Jesus took it from there.

Then a group of Greeks, those considered by the disciples to be outside the scope of Christ's kingdom interests, came to Philip. Philip told Andrew. Andrew's quiet wisdom convinced Philip they ought to bring the Greeks to Jesus.

Andrew's life style isn't very dramatic. You'd probably put him among the plodders, those who quietly without any fuss do what needs to be done. Andrew wouldn't be comfortable as a dramatic front-and-center-stage preacher like his brother Peter. He'd rather be involved in helping others, of thinking how to bring people into contact with Christ.

Do not underestimate the quiet drama of such a life. It has excitement whether or not the person realizes it.

How the church needs its Andrews! Without them little will be accomplished. They save the church from becoming a company of spectators. Healthy, robust Andrews are always finding someone or something to bring to Christ.

It's the Andrews in an average congregation who get the work done. They quietly roll up their sleeves and do the needed work. If the Andrews weren't around, the world would know little of the compassionate interest of God's people in dying men.

Roll up your sleeves. The Lord is looking for more volunteers for the Royal Order of Andrew.

FOR DISCUSSION

1. We have no record of Andrew witnessing about Christ except to invite Peter to "come and hear." Does this mean he wasn't a witness? Must one verbalize his faith in Christ or quote Scripture to be a witness? Discuss thoroughly.
2. Can we "bring a person to Christ" without some verbal witness? Explain.

3. We often condemn those who do not verbalize their faith. Do we have scriptural support for such an attitude? How can such people be helped to be more expressive?
4. Does your church make an adequate place for those who find their niche to be a caring witness rather than a verbal witness? How is this specifically emphasized?
5. Being like Andrew is not an excuse to be quiet. How can one open up in his witness for Christ?
6. Are there ever times when we talk too much? When we are more like Peter than like Andrew? What are the results?
7. What analytical characteristics did Andrew possess? How can these be developed? How were they put to good use by Christ?

9. Contradictions

He asked his disciples, "Who do men say that the Son of man is?" And they said, "Some say John the Baptist, others say Elijah, and others Jeremiah or one of the prophets." He said to them, "But who do you say that I am?" Simon Peter replied, "You are the Christ, the Son of the living God" (Matt. 16:13-16). ... After a little while the bystanders came up and said to Peter, "Certainly you are also one of them, for your accent betrays you." Then he began to invoke a curse on himself and to swear, "I do not know the man" (Matt. 16:73, 74).

And Jesus answered him, "Blessed are you, Simon Bar-Jona! For flesh and blood has not revealed this to you, but my Father who is in heaven. And I tell you, you are Peter, and on this rock I will build my church, and the powers of death shall not prevail against it. I will give you the keys of the kingdom of heaven" (Matt. 16:17-19).

... But he turned and said to Peter, "Get behind me Satan! You are a hindrance to me; for you are not on the side of God, but of men" (Matt. 16:23).

No one disputes Peter's primacy among the first twelve disciples of Christ. He was No. 1. Even the gospel writers gave him that place of prominence. Whenever they listed the most important disciples, Peter's name came first. Jesus selected him as a member of the Peter, James and John trio. When Jairus' daughter died, Jesus "allowed no one to follow him except Peter and James and John" (Mark 5:37). "Jesus took with him Peter and James and John, and led them up a high mountain apart by themselves; and he was transfigured before them" (Mark 9:2). "And they went to a place which is called Gethsemane; and he said to his disciples, 'Sit here while I pray.' And he took with him Peter and James and John, and began to be greatly distressed and troubled (Mark 14:32, 33).

Peter came up with the poignant, theology-packed proclamation that identified Jesus as the Christ. The other disciples simply reported what others were saying about the Savior. But Peter stoutly declared, "You are the Christ, the Son of the living God."

On another occasion he asked a sincere question which revealed the depth of his thinking. "Lord, how often shall my brother sin against me, and I forgive him? As many as seven times?" (Matt. 18:21).

Jesus praised Peter for his spiritual insight. Then Christ uttered one of the most controversial passages in the New Testament. These words about Peter have led many (including the entire Roman Catholic Church) to interpret Christ's remarks to mean that he would build the entire church on Peter.

Overagainst these defenses of Peter's supremacy, his allegiance to Christ, his theological understanding, his bravery, we discover another Peter.

Here the theological whiz doesn't know what he's talking about. After being among the favored trio on the Mount of Transfiguration, Peter proposes, "Master, it is well that we are here; let us make three booths, one for you and one for Moses and one for Elijah—not knowing what he said" (Luke 9:33). That last phrase reveals something about the unexplainable contradiction in the chiefest of the twelve.

Recorded in the same chapter as his Messiah proclamation is his attempt to rebuke Jesus for talking about his coming Calvary encounter. Jesus used strong language to set Peter straight, "Get behind me, Satan!

You are a hindrance to me; for you are not on the side of God, but of men" (Matt. 16:23).

When Peter was invited along with the other two of the favored trio to share in the agony of Gethsemane, he fell asleep. "And he came and found them sleeping, and he said to Peter, 'Simon, are you asleep? Could you not watch one hour?' " (Mark 14:37).

His bravery collapsed when Jesus was on trial and a few insignificant people accused him of being a disciple of Christ. Reread the shocking words of Matthew 26:73, 74. He even began to curse and swear to prove he had no connections with Jesus Christ.

John 21:3 describes another shocking activity of the great man. You'd expect the leader of the group to be thinking about the resurrection. But Peter wasn't impressed. He told Thomas and Nathanael, "I'm going fishing." You couldn't find a more serious time to suggest such a frivolous activity.

Hundreds of sermons have been preached on the character of Peter. To be fair to him we must recognize his strengths as well as his weaknesses. But as we review the character of this man we are puzzled. Why such unexplainable contradictions?

Twentieth-century Peters? Many—and just as amazing. Both within and outside the church we have witnessed many people who seem so strong, aggressive, and possess true leadership qualities. And then suddenly these people display a character weakness and the high estimation we've had of them topples. Former president Richard Nixon is a showcase example.

When we see glaring contradictions in the lives of biblical characters, we are often thrown. We've usually pictured only their strengths. We've concluded that we have to possess those strong characteristics before God can use us. Somehow the biblical people were extraordinary persons. Then when we take a closer look at their activities and beliefs we are shocked. Peter wasn't different from us. We too have had our moments of bravery, of intellectual proclamation, of forward witness. And we've also had our moments of denial, frivolous activity, poor judgment.

Maybe James understood human personality quite clearly when he wrote about another biblical character who had unexplainable contradictions within: "Elijah was a man subject to like passion as ourselves" (James 5:17, KJV).

FOR DISCUSSION

1. Recall some of Peter's strong characteristics. How did these work to his benefit? to his detriment? in service to Jesus Christ?
2. Why would Christ choose a man whose personality possessed such contradictory characteristics. Why would he become a leader?
3. How does a personal relationship/commitment to Jesus Christ minimize such conflicting characteristics? Be specific in your answer.
4. Can any person justify the continuance of conflicting characteristics? Should he be discouraged with himself? What hope does such a person have?
5. How should we react to others who seem to possess unexplainable contradictory characteristics?
6. What can be done on a personal basis to improve the positive and eliminate the negative aspects of our characters.
8. Give any examples which show how God uses both types of characteristics within a person. Are all our contradictory negatives sinful and in need of being confessed and transformed? Explain.

10. Making Performance Match Beliefs

And as he sat at table in the house, behold, many tax collectors and sinners came and sat down with Jesus and his disciples. And when the Pharisees saw this, they said to his disciples, "Why does your teacher eat with tax collectors and sinners?" But when he heard it, he said, "Those who are well have no need of a physician, but those who are sick, Go and learn what this means, 'I desire mercy, and not sacrifice.' For I came not to call the righteous, but sinners" (Matt. 9:10-13).

A Pharisee asked him to dine with him; so he went and sat at table. The Pharisee was astonished to see that he did not first wash before dinner. And the Lord said to him, "Now you Pharisees cleanse the outside of the cup and of the dish, but inside you are full of extortion and wickedness" (Luke: 37-39).

... he began to say to his disciples first, "Beware of the leaven of the Pharisees, which is hypocrisy. Nothing is covered up that will not be revealed, or hidden that will not be known. Whatever you have said in the dark shall be heard in the light, and whatever you have whispered in private rooms shall be proclaimed upon the housetops (Luke 12:1-3).

Even a junior higher can give a rather accurate definition of a Pharisee: a fellow who claims to be religious but doesn't live up to what he says. A Pharisee in today's evangelical circles would be a good Bible verse quoter, able to rattle off all the requirements for church membership, and present at almost every church service. But

Scripture quoted in this chapter is from the New International Version unless otherwise indicated.

. . . the Pharisee's everyday life and actions fail to reflect all those Bible quotes and the hours spent in church on Sunday.

When Jesus came in conflict with the Pharisees, or vice versa, it was at this very point. The Pharisees were known as "righteous" people. They met all the standards of the law. In our language they were "spiritual" people. So why did Jesus have such harsh things to say about them? Didn't he recognize their adherence to the law? Didn't he know of their religious practices?

There are no passages in the New Testament which depict the Pharisees in a good light. While their reputation as being righteous and religious pops out in almost every one of the Gospels, yet the impression given is that they are not the ones after which to model our lives. In fact, Jesus declared that "unless your righteousness exceeds that of the scribes and Pharisees, you will never enter the kingdom of heaven" (Matt. 5:20).

Why was Jesus so hard on the Pharisees? He said that he came not to destroy but to fulfill the law. Wasn't the practice of the law by the Pharisees a fulfillment of that law? Why did he condemn them at every turn?

Examine a few more of the incidents in which the Pharisees encountered Christ and came out on the losing end:

In Matthew 12:1-8 the disciples plucked ears of grain and ate on the sabbath. To the Pharisee this was unlawful. Jesus explained that God desired mercy and not sacrifice and "the Son of man is lord of the sabbath."

In the same chapter (vv. 12:9-14) he met their challenge of "Is it lawful to heal on the sabbath?" by restoring a man's withered hand. Recording this incident, Luke (6:9) adds the question of the Savior, "I ask you, is it lawful on the sabbath to do good or to do harm, to save life or to destroy it?"

Luke 11:37-41 records the incident of a Pharisee asking Jesus to dinner. Jesus didn't wash before eating. This shocked the self-righteous Pharisee who had made washing hands before eating a religious practice. Jesus looked at him and talked about the outside of the cup being polished and clean while the inside of the cup was full of extortion and wickedness. Ouch, that hurt!

Matthew 23 and Luke 11 contain some of the harshest words our Lord ever uttered. He pointed his finger straight at the noses of the Pharisees and cried, "Woe unto you, scribes and Pharisees, hypocrites!" It wasn't a single outburst of anger but seven well-thought out condemnations. Their ears and hearts were blistered.

Probably the severest criticism of the Pharisees comes in Christ's mildly stated conclusion: "So you also outwardly appear righteous to men, but within you are full of hypocrisy and iniquity" (Matt. 23:28).

Twentieth-century Christianity isn't free from phariseeism. Far too often today's Christians have all the outward signs of righteousness. We mouth the correct clichés. We don't attend x-rated movies. We have regulations concerning Sunday activities. We attend church whenever the doors swing open. We quote Scripture verses when we explain our beliefs to non-Christians or when we attempt to win them. Yet the world knows us more by our practices than our preachments. We often concentrate on doctrinal positions and truths and neglect the effect those doctrines must have on our daily activities. We are right doctrinally but as someone has said, "We have our dispensations all right but our dispositions all wrong." The Pharisees had that problem too.

The sad plight of the Pharisees was that they were completely unaware of their hypocrisy. They felt they were in the right. They were obeying the laws. It was Christ and his disciples who were out of line.

That's the way it is with anyone who maintains a

religious reputation. He steeps himself in all the proper beliefs and words and fails to realize that God and others measure his religion by performance as well as belief. In the final judgment we shall give account for our attitudes and practices as well as for our doctrines.

Matching one's performance to his beliefs demands a lot of honest practice as well as belief.

FOR DISCUSSION

1. Name some of the good characteristics of the Pharisees.
2. Why did Jesus have so many confrontations with "religious" people? Why do we have so little record of his conflicts with the "non-religious" (except for Pilate)?
3. Does the condemnation of the outwardness of Pharisaic religion tell us anything about religious practices today? Of what must we be cautious? What must we avoid?
4. Why is it so difficult to perform in accordance to the truths of one's religion? How can one be doctrinally correct yet so out of sorts dispositionally?
5. How does one avoid becoming a hypocrite?
6. Do churches unconsciously promote hypocrisy by making it easy to believe and to verbalize one's beliefs? How can this be remedied?
7. What responsibility does an individual have when he suspects another Christian of hypocrisy? How should he counsel the other person?
8. Since hypocrisy is difficult to discover within oneself and even more difficult to admit, how can a person avoid falling into its trap?

11. Curious or Committed

He entered Jericho and was passing through. And there was a man named Zacchaeus; he was a chief tax collector, and rich. And he sought to see who Jesus was, but could not, on account of the crowd, because he was small in stature. So he ran on ahead and climbed up into a sycamore tree to see him, for he was to pass that way. And when Jesus came to the place, he looked up and said to him, "Zacchaeus, make haste and come down; for I must stay at your house today." So he made haste and came down, and received him joyfully . . . And Zacchaeus stood and said to the Lord, "Behold, Lord, the half of my goods I give to the poor; and if I have defrauded any one of anything I restore it fourfold." And Jesus said to him, "Today salvation has come to this house, since he also is a son of Abraham. For the Son of Man came to seek and to save the lost" (Luke 19:1-10).

From earliest childhood many of us have sung "Zacchaeus was a wee little man, a wee little man was he. He climbed into a sycamore tree, for the Lord he wanted to see. And as the Savior passed that way, he said, 'Zacchaeus, you come down. For I'm going to your house today!' " We went through several motions as we sang, showing Zacchaeus looking down and the Lord looking up. The whole presentation concentrates on the curiosity generated. The artwork in Sunday school booklets have also created this impression. Zacchaeus was curious to see and meet Jesus and he had his curiosity satisfied.

The satisfaction of curiosity has played a part in much religious observance. Picture the scene at the garden tomb on the morning of the resurrection (John 20:1-8). Peter came with the other disciple to the tomb. The other disciple "reached the tomb first; and stooping to look in, he saw the linen cloth lying there, but he did not go in" (vv. 4, 5). That wasn't enough to satisfy the more curious Peter. "He went into the tomb . . ." (v.6).

Curiosity attracted Moses to heed the call of God. "Moses said, 'I will turn aside and see this great sight, why the bush is not burnt.' When the Lord saw that he turned aside to see, God called to him out of the bush" (Exod. 3:3, 4). The Lord highly honored Moses' curiosity. Without the desire to see what was going on at the unconsumed bush, he could have missed God's call.

A certain amount of curiosity is necessary to excite one to discovery. This is true in almost every area of life. Those who aren't inquisitive lead more or less dull lives. Those who are always examining possibilities have more exciting experiences.

This can also be applied to the Christian life. A healthy curiosity can lead a person into a fresher and more intimate acquaintance with Christ. If one is satisfied to make no more than a few superficial discoveries, his life will be lived on a superficial level.

Of course, there can be an unhealthy curiosity. The person who seems to look continually for new experiences but does not pursue them in any depth has become a victim of curiosity. He can be seen visiting several churches to enjoy special programs. He can be seen going from one religious meeting to another just to see what's going on. The satisfaction of curiosity is the highest, although unconscious, goal of his church-hopping.

The curiosity which leads one in the direction Zacchaeus went is most desirable. Jesus wanted to go to Zacchaeus' house. And in the home situation Zacchaeus spelled out his commitment to right living. He "made haste and came down, and received him [Christ] joyfully." His intent was far more than to have his curiosity satisfied. But his curiosity (we might even call it a sanctified curiosity) led him to a great and satisfying encounter with the Master. Curiosity led to commitment.

Let's not forget this aspect of the Zacchaeus/Jesus encounter. Zacchaeus made clear his intentions. His commitment showed a morality unknown of his kind. And it was a commitment that cost. As a tax collector he went beyond any law. He could hold his head high as he told Jesus, "The half of my goods I give to the poor; and if I have defrauded anyone (a common practice by the tax collectors) of anything, I restore it fourfold."

Curiosity led Zacchaeus to Jesus, but commitment soon followed. And the immediate response of Jesus was, "Today salvation has come to this house, since he also is a son of Abraham. For the Son of man came to seek and to save the lost." What clearer explanation could Christ give concerning a converted man?

If curiosity produces such results, it would be well to plan programs in the twentieth-century church which would arouse curiosity. If people who come out of curiosity make commitments, then it's time the church takes advantage of curiosity. But if we get only onlookers, the producers of the curious event are as guilty as those who seek satisfaction without commitment.

FOR DISCUSSION

1. Review what the Bible says about Zacchaeus. What descriptions make him a good candidate for only being curious? What could lead you to believe he was earnestly searching?
2. Could we say that curiosity is a gift from God? Explain. What are its values?
3. Is there enough in your local church's program to excite outsiders to come out of curiosity? If not, should there be?

4. In a world of electronically produced entertainments and curiosities, how should the church compete? How do we attract outsiders?
5. What are some dangers in developing a program that attracts the curious? How can these dangers be avoided?
6. How can we lead a person from the realm of curiosity into a position of commitment?
7. If we have been guilty of formulating programs that promote superficial commitments, what should be done to correct this? How can we inspire more wholehearted, Zacchaeus-type commitments?
8. Where does the lordship of Christ fit into this discussion? Would a call to submission to his lordship correct the problems of satisfying the more superficial aspects of curiosity?

12. A New Direction

My manner of life from my youth, spent from the beginning among my own nation and at Jerusalem, is known by all the Jews. They have known for a long time, if they are willing to testify, that according to the strictest party of our religion I have lived as a Pharisee. And now I stand here on trial for hope in the promise made by God to our fathers.... I myself was convinced that I ought to do many things in opposing the name of Jesus of Nazareth. And I did so in Jerusalem; I not only shut up many of the saints in prison, by authority of the chief priests, but when they were put to death I cast my vote against them. And I punished them often in synagogues and tried to make them blaspheme; and in raging fury against them, I persecuted them even to foreign cities (Acts 26:4-11).

But whatever gain I had, I counted as loss for the sake of Christ. Indeed I count everything a loss because of the surpassing worth of knowing Christ Jesus my Lord. For his sake I have suffered the loss of all things, and count them as refuse, in order that I may gain Christ and be found in him, not having a righteousness of my own, based on law, but that which is through faith in Christ, the righteousness from God that depends on faith; that I may know him and the power of his resurrection, and may share his suffering, becoming like him in his death, that if possible I may attain the resurrection from the dead (Phil. 3:7-11).

Whenever we look for a classic example of conversion we quickly name the apostle Paul or John Newton, the converted slave trader who wrote the famous hymn "Amazing Grace." If asked why we so readily identify such people, it seems easy to explain. These people gave evidence of fitting the meaning of conversion—being turned in a new direction.

An examination of Paul's encounter with Christ on the Damascus highway gives clear indication of how his life turned in new directions. It seems necessary to spell out what he turned from as well as what he turned to. So let's examine the first mention of Paul's conversion in Acts 9:1-22.

First, Paul immediately recognized Jesus Christ. This is the beginning point of conversion. His conversion didn't begin at the point which Peter indicated in his Pentecostal sermon, "Repent" (Acts 2:14-38). Of course, Paul had previous knowledge of who Jesus was claimed to be. He was able to identify those who followed in the ways of Christ. He'd mark them for his particular mode of persecution "breathing out threats and murder against the disciples of the Lord."

But Paul's acceptance of the Christian religion was much more than mere knowledge of who Jesus Christ was. It was a recognition of who Jesus was in relationship to the person Paul. That made all the difference. Paul had a personal encounter with Christ. That encounter resulted in an immediate turning away from Paul's normal activities.

Probably one of the strongest evidences of conversion can be found by examining one's activities. As these are discovered to be contrary to the teachings of Scripture, one turns away from them. In the case of Paul, since there was such a contrast between his persecuting ventures and his acceptance of Christ, the turning had to be as dramatic as either his activity or his faith. The principle holds true: any activity in opposition to God's ways must be relinquished.

A second evidence of Paul's conversion was his resultant mild spirit. The first verse of the text indicates a ferocious attitude, "breathing out threats and murders." The stunning encounter on the Damascus highway humbled the proud persecutor. He willingly submitted to being led into the city. After receiving his sight three days later he submitted to Christian baptism. His change of attitude is also evident from the comments of those who heard him talk about Jesus. They were amazed and said, "Is not this the man who made havoc in Jerusalem of those who called on this name? And he has come here for this purpose" (Acts 9:21).

Another evidence of his conversion was his choice of friends. He had come to Damascus with a group who hated the name of Christ. Now he openly identifies himself with those who proclaim allegiance to the Savior. He had come with considerable authority. He joins those who were despised. He spent several days in Damascus, even going into the synagogues, to proclaim his identity with Christ and Christ's followers. So well did he make this switch into the Christian community that in a few days the Jewish community plotted to kill him (Acts 9:23).

Paul's later life gives adequate evidence that his conversion experience on the Damascus road was genuine. No matter where we encounter him, in Acts or in the epistles he penned, we can see that his life was under new management.

To understand conversion in our time, and to have assurance on a personal basis, we can still look for evidences of turning. The Christian way, even when it is accepted by a morally acceptable individual, still results in some turnings, especially from a self-willed walk.

Paul's conversion was the result of a dramatic, emotion-packed encounter. This does not mean all conversions take place in like manner. Study the lives of Mark, Timothy or Lydia and you'll not find much drama. Yet they were people whose lives had been turned into the Way. Most of us can be grateful for such examples in the Bible.

FOR DISCUSSION

1. Would you describe conversion more as a turning or a turning around? Why?
2. While some conversions are dramatic, what are the dangers of expecting a dramatic encounter?
3. How can an emphasis on conversion as dramatic encounter cause problems for people on the brink of a decision?
4. Discuss some of the evidences you have discovered within yourself that assure you that you were converted. Were there accompanying outward evidences? Should there be?
5. The complaint often heard is that many who profess faith in Christ now seem dead on the vine. Why does this seem to be so? Is there fault in our presentation of the message of Christ? How can this be changed?
6. Why would a stronger emphasis on the lordship of Jesus Christ help to make stronger converts? Can this be done without making it too difficult to believe?
7. To what extent should we look for outward manifestations of one's inner experience? Can we zero in on any of these manifestations?
8. How have your relationships with others changed because you are converted? Should conversion force one to withdraw from society? Why, or why not?
9. You know many people who need to be converted. How do you go about helping them to have life-changing encounters with Christ?

13. Thank Quotients

On the way to Jerusalem he was passing along between Samaria and Galilee. And as he entered a village, he was met by ten lepers, who stood at a distance and lifted up their voices and said, "Jesus, Master, have mercy on us." When he saw them he said to them, "Go and show yourselves to the priests." And as they went they were cleansed. Then one of them... turned back, praising God with a loud voice; and he fell on his face at Jesus, feet, giving him thanks. Now he was a Samaritan. Then said Jesus, "Were not ten cleansed? Where are the nine? Was no one found to return and give praise to God except this foreigner?" (Luke 17:11-18).

Give thanks in all circumstances; for this is the will of God in Christ Jesus for you (I Thess. 5:18).

Most of us can recall childhood experiences when we forgot to thank someone for a gift or favor. Our parents embarrassed us by asking, "Did you say thanks?" If we hadn't said the magic words, we were sent back while the person was still present. With bowed head we muttered "Thank you" and they replied, "That's all right." Later one of our parents reprimanded us, "The next time you forget, you're not getting the gift!" But even the scolding didn't seem to ingrain thankfulness into our vocabulary or our spirit. When the opportunity arose to say the magic words, we forgot the formula. And, you guessed it, our parents repeated the same shame routine.

Lest we conclude that this is only a characteristic of untrained children, let's examine our own attitudes and

Scripture passages in this section are from the American Standard Version unless otherwise indicated.

experiences. Maybe we'll discover we're more like the nine lepers than like No.10.

As we consider Luke's account of this incident, we can discover several excellent reasons why all ten men ought to have come back to praise God.

First, Jesus paid particular attention to a despised minority group. Lepers were the outcasts of society. Healthy people wouldn't touch them or even come near them. Society demanded that they live outside the village limits. The proud, physically washed Jews associated leprosy with sin.

When Jesus paid particular attention to the lepers, they were honored. Others despised them; he loved them. Others drove them away; he would call them to himself. Wouldn't this spark at least an attitude, if not the words, of thankfulness?

Secondly, Jesus cured all ten of them of life's then known greatest malady—leprosy. It was one disease from which few ever recovered, except via miracle. Jesus performed that miracle and sent them to the priests to confirm it. Now they could re-enter normal society. Now they could fellowship with their family members. Now they could throw away their begging paraphernalia. Now they could participate in the full regalia of their religion. Wasn't all this more than enough to cause them to walk many miles to verbalize their thankfulness to the healer?

Luke tells us that only one returned. He was a foreigner, a Samaritan (one probably despised by the leprous Jews). He was the one no one would expect to return.

No. 10 didn't care who heard his words of thanks. He "turned back, praising God with a loud voice; and he fell on his face at Jesus' feet, giving him thanks." He was unashamed of his emotional outbursts. What did he care about others' evaluations of his joy? He was full of joy.

He couldn't keep it inside. He worshiped the healer. He showed his thankfulness as well as shouted it.

Jesus questioned, "Were not ten cleansed? Where are the nine? Was no one found to return to give praise to God except this foreigner?" The nine had received the same benefits as No. 10. They probably told others and the priests that they had been cured by Jesus. Their re-entry into society was contingent upon their report to the priests. Among themselves and within the thinking of each of these former lepers, they probably expressed the fact, "Thank God, I'm cured!"

This opens several areas of thought concerning thankfulness. Begin with the lack of verbal expression. In many cases we probably get into situations such as that in which the lepers were involved. Something great happened because of an encounter with another person, yet we didn't verbalize.

Possibly verbalization was a matter of inconvenience. We would have to go out of our way to express thanks. Possibly we couldn't relocate the person who did us the favor. So in typical fashion we eased our conscience by uttering a generalized prayer for everything good that came to us.

Often a lack of verbal expression is caused by something deeper than inconvenience. These lepers could have been taking the hard knocks of society for quite some time. Unconsciously they felt it was about time they got a big break. Now it came—exactly what they deserved. So what's the big deal about going back to the healer with a warm thank you note? It's not the usual practice for a patient (even in the 1970s) to make much ado about being cured after taking six or seven hundred capsules.

Unexpressed thanks can also reveal a thankless heart. If the nine felt they were getting what they deserved, they'd take all the good they could get. They may have thought they deserved back pay for all the time they spent in the leper colony. Up to this point they had been cheated out of much life. Now life was paying them back.

Before we severely condemn the nine, let's be sure to check our own thank quotient. Recall situations in which we verbalized our thanks. Recall other situations in which we would have been inconvenienced or possibly embarrassed if we said thank you. We made a mental note to express thanks at a future time (more convenient to us) but that time seemed to stretch beyond a wise limit. Maybe the recipient of the intended thanks was already saying to himself, "He never said thanks for what I did for him."

Now let's look at the second verse of our text: "Give thanks in all circumstances; for this is the will of God in Christ Jesus for you." This is a challenge—especially for those who do not glibly recite Romans 8:28, "we know that in everything God works for good with those who love him." For the person who sincerely struggles with this, verbalization for adverse circumstances presents many problems, but especially the problem of unrealistic wording.

Giving thanks in **all** circumstances might be expressed only to God in the inner struggles of prayer wrestling. Yet we need to approach this. Recognizing the difficulty involved does not negate reaching toward the ideal.

Without debating all the philosophical and theological questions involved, we can turn to another aspect of thankfulness. All of us can improve on the thanks we express toward others. Rather than being the exception or an awkward practice, saying thanks can become a norm.

FOR DISCUSSION

1. Does the adage "much blessing, much thanks" hold true in light of our text? Why, or why not?

2. Can we justify the silence of the nine cleansed lepers? Were they worthy of healing? Why, or why not?
3. Why are we often reticent in expressing thanks? How can this be overcome?
4. Are generalized "thank you" words to God accepted? Why is it difficult to be specific?
5. Have you ever encountered a person who seems too thankful? What seems to motivate over-expression? How do you analyze such an encounter?
6. Would you say that some thanks, as described in I Thessalonians 5:18, can be expressed only to God, or will they be reserved in expression even then? Explain. How can one be thankful in adversity without being unrealistic?
7. Give examples of times in life when thanks needs to be withheld or postponed.
8. How can you make sure the recipient detects the sincerity of your thanks?
9. Does a pessimistic outlook on the immediate future of the world hinder thanksgiving? How can this be brought in line with Christian reality?
10. How can we develop thankfulness more as an attitude toward all of life rather than merely an expression because of specific objects or experiences?
11. The apostle Paul gives no expression of thanks for his personal gains in Christ (such as his own salvation) but continually thanks God for others. What does this say about one's prayer life? Is it an example to follow? How can it be developed?